ENDURE. BE. ADAPT.

ENDURE.

BE.

ADAPT.

by Daniel Rugon

Cracow 2019

© Copyright by Daniel Rugon, 2019

Illustrations and cover graphic

© Copyright by Julia Piwowarczyk, 2019

All rights reserved. No part of this publication may be reproduced, distributed, or transmitted in any form or by any means, including photocopying, recording, or other electronic or mechanical methods, without the prior written permission of the publisher, except in the case of brief quotations embodied in critical reviews and certain other noncommercial uses permitted by copyright law. For permission requests, write to the publisher, addressed "Request for Permissions" at the address below.

rugon.daniel.88@gmail.com

ISBN 978-83-953518-0-8

ISBN 978-83-953518-1-5

ENDURANCE

Chill

Between the worlds it exists

Reminding of its presence to us

I'm not sure whether it's a pacifist

As in mind it creates a fuss.

What is this ghastly shade

To which feelings awake

What had it previously made

To be nor real nor fake?

The chill runs down the spine

Kindly reminding of dues to pay

Is it punishment or divine?

For sure, bodies in coffin lay.

The fate of yours is not done yet

Do not forget what you have done

In the end, you deserve and get;

Let the soul be saved and NOT begone!

Pitch Black

The sight filled with reds, yellows and blues

Full of scents, filling the lungs and caves

Textures giving fingertips clues

Wild waves and sound behaves.

All of such rich and vast

Attack the mind to thrive

The world's image is cast

Should you feel alive!

And yet all is rebounced

Reaching only the shell

Echo is lost announced

Fog of NONE here fell.

The body of red dwarf

Hides in a tiny figure

Feelings are like twarf

One neutron no bigger.

The googolfold gravity

Loneliness ball

Soul's depravity

Me in black hole.

Desire or Gratefulness Lost

All sins are acquired

Through struggles and pains

More and more is required

Just to count the gains.

Humans want more power

As all sin lies in desire

It's the mother of doom

But will you listen to whom?

— No matter the cost, forget the past

  Do it now! That's the first – Lust.

— With more objects, mind will be freed

  Yet it's tangled and moored in Greed.

— No action, only the words and an oath

  This is the only and true name of Sloth.

— They are together, make bloodbath

  Don't be stopped and unleash Wrath.

— There's the treasure chest, mine's the key

  They cannot have more, I'm coated in Envy.

— Raise your head high while you stride

  As a final fall is proceeded with Pride.

Listening and Hearing

Hearing the words of the other

Spoken utterly from mind and heart

Makes some consider it a bother

And let the good man be torn apart,

Hearing the words of the other

Not letting them to be listened

It's the prime sin against our Father

As the blood on his son's sides glistened,

Hearing the words of the other

Is not letting Him be heard

Only understanding you're my brother

And then you can become a bird.

Needs

Just water and food

A shelter safe and sound

With parents, it's all good

In parental love bound

But if one is greedy like hell

Clawing for more and more

It's all in vain; anyone can tell

Children get spoiled, adore no more

Money and goods corrupt the soul

Giving not love but pure pain

You cannot become whole

If you only want to gain

Emotions

Deep inside

Chemical compound

Unknown to

Scientists

Governing the body

The Mind

The Living

***

Defining

Undefinable

By experience

Of pace

Mountain river

Low and stream

It goes

***

Positive

Negative

Tear squeezing

Face – tearing

All surface

Up from

The inside

The reflection

The mirror is to act

Put a mask on

Create new fact

A play-out con

Mirror teaches

Product maker

Reflection preaches

Just a faker

Truth knows

No lies

It shows

In the eyes

EXISTENCE

The Word

Lone symbols cluster and flow

They freely leave a hand and go

These are put together in a line

Trying to mesmerise mind of thyne

Yet be aware of dualism there

Words are powerful, but pay a fare

They can spread poison far and wide

But in the end the truth will abide.

The Mind Weather

The mental stability

Like mountain weather

Changes credibility

To worse or better

Insignificant grain

Can tip the scale

Ravage the brain

Make you pale

Bright golden ray

Rises the morale

No need to say

The peak is final

To be victorious

Balance is the key

In universe glorious

Always pay the fee

The Age

The calmness of move

The swiftness of mind

Nothing left to prove

'The only' of its kind

Wrinkles cascade in layers

Each carrying experience

More and more prayers

To fill the inexperience

Eyes dimmingly shine

With burden and power

It's the time sign

That's sweet and sour

The flow of toothless words

Hardly falls down beard

Yet these will lead herds

Like prophets seem(ed) weird

It shapes the wise

Making them much humble

But the stupid dies

Perishes with crumble

The Sun

Bulbs and lamps

Neons and leds

All shining bright

Above our heads

They give light

And sense of security

But civilised humanity

Is left in obscurity

This false light

Which is truly fake

Harms our eyesight

And makes the head ache

The only one Sun

Holding ancient power

Gives everything the life

And will everything devour

Copy of a Copy

Created ages ago

It still lasts unchanged

Thinking it's new though

That's stagnation revenge

Presented with emotion

Charismatically spoken

The image of devotion

Waiting for gratitude token

The speech is repeated

All over again and again

Speaker feels unbeaten

Yet it's just in vain

The era of multiplying

Spreading copies of copies

Is presenting this satisfying?

Silly, boring copies ...

Artists' Path

Strolling down the insanity

Existence disperses in all

Leave behind the vanity

To hear the highest call

Still anchored in reality

You are creation bridge

One false step to fatality

Never cross the ridge

Schizophrenic mind in all great

Allows them to come and go

Stay too long, play with fate

Your body shattered, arched in bow

Pen

Tracing the thought

Conveying the mind

Signs together brought

Some lose, some find

Tips stained in ink

Thus the mind flows

Ones forget to blink

The hand always knows

Memories fly away

Alzheimer is close

To keep thoughts at bay

Pour into paper those

ADAPTATION

INTRODUCTION

Airport

or Minimalism Flew Away

All the suitcases thrust

All travellers tense

All there's croissants' crust

All the continental hence

No one's taken just a few

No one has just a list

No one looks true

No one s a minimalist

The garden of St. Joseph

or Rock Waterfall

The liquid's dripping

My heart's gripping

While seated near

Cleansed of fear

The rhythmic drop

As heard non-stop

Splashes my lids

And spirit needs

The Saints above

Pray to Love

While birds abathe

In purest faith

My sanctuary's strong

I'm not in wrong

The path lies ahead

Faith, water and bread

Writer's Workshop

Just a pen

And a note

Write then

To promote

Just a lamp

And a desk

Ink stamp

Paper fresc

Just a few

Not too many

Enough for you

Earn a penny

Yet the mind

And the spirit

Work to find

What's "in it"

In the dark

Ink scribes

As morning lark

Visionary bribes

The initiation

The flow

The creation

White Crow

The Moss

Tiny tundras on each hair

Packed tightly like summer train

Each in family of love and care

Scientists say simple without brain

See them wise even though small

Grow slowly and mesmerisingly

Catching the bark on trees crawl

Tough and lasting, surprisingly

Individual in green shades

Sprout and quarter-inch jump

All the diversity here fades

All united hold and clamp

The moss is fine

It contains time

Wisdom of eternity

Nature in simplicity

The Maze

or **The Brain**

Paths twist

They swirl

In the mist

In the twirl

They go up

And go down

Make a map

Make a town

A stronghold

A fortification

Thinking bold

In unification

Tree Bark

Piece to piece

Skin to skin

Natural fleece

Of my kin

It protects

It cures

It reflects

It pures

Grows thick

Gets strong

Solid brick

Ancient Kong

Art Cafe

The place is here

We're sitting

Drinking beer

Coffee sipping

The place is here

Reading book

Without fear

Content look

The place is here

No other

No tear

No bother

Contents

ENDURANCE..5
   Chill..7
   Pitch Black...8
   Desire or Gratefulness Lost....................10
   Listening and Hearing............................12
   Needs...13
   Emotions..14
   The reflection..16

EXISTENCE..19
   The Word...21
   The Mind Weather..................................22
   The Age..24
   The Sun..26
   Copy of a Copy......................................28
   Artists' Path..30
   Pen..31

ADAPTATION..35
   Airport..37
   or Minimalism Flew Away......................37
   The garden of St. Joseph.........................38
   or Rock Waterfall....................................38
   Writer's Workshop..................................40
   The Moss..42
   The Maze..44
   or The Brain...44
   Tree Bark..45
   Art Cafe..46

www.ingramcontent.com/pod-product-compliance
Lightning Source LLC
Chambersburg PA
CBHW060542030426
42337CB00021B/4399